Adapted by Margaret Snyder
Illustrated by Darrell Baker

MERRIGOLD PRESS • NEW YORK
© 1994 The Walt Disney Company. All rights reserved. Printed in the U.S.A. No part of this book may be reproduced or copied in any form without written permission from the copyright owner. MERRIGOLD PRESS® and MERRIGOLD PRESS & DESIGN™ are the property of Merrigold Press, New York, New York 10022. Library of Congress Catalog Card Number: 94-78271 ISBN: 0-307-11171-7 A MCMXCIV

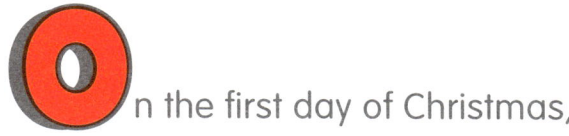

On the first day of Christmas,

Goofy gave to me

A partridge in a square tree.

On the second day of Christmas,

Minnie gave to me

Two dancing gloves,

And a partridge in a square tree.

On the third day of Christmas,

Donald gave to me

Three feather pens,

Two dancing gloves,

And a partridge in a square tree.

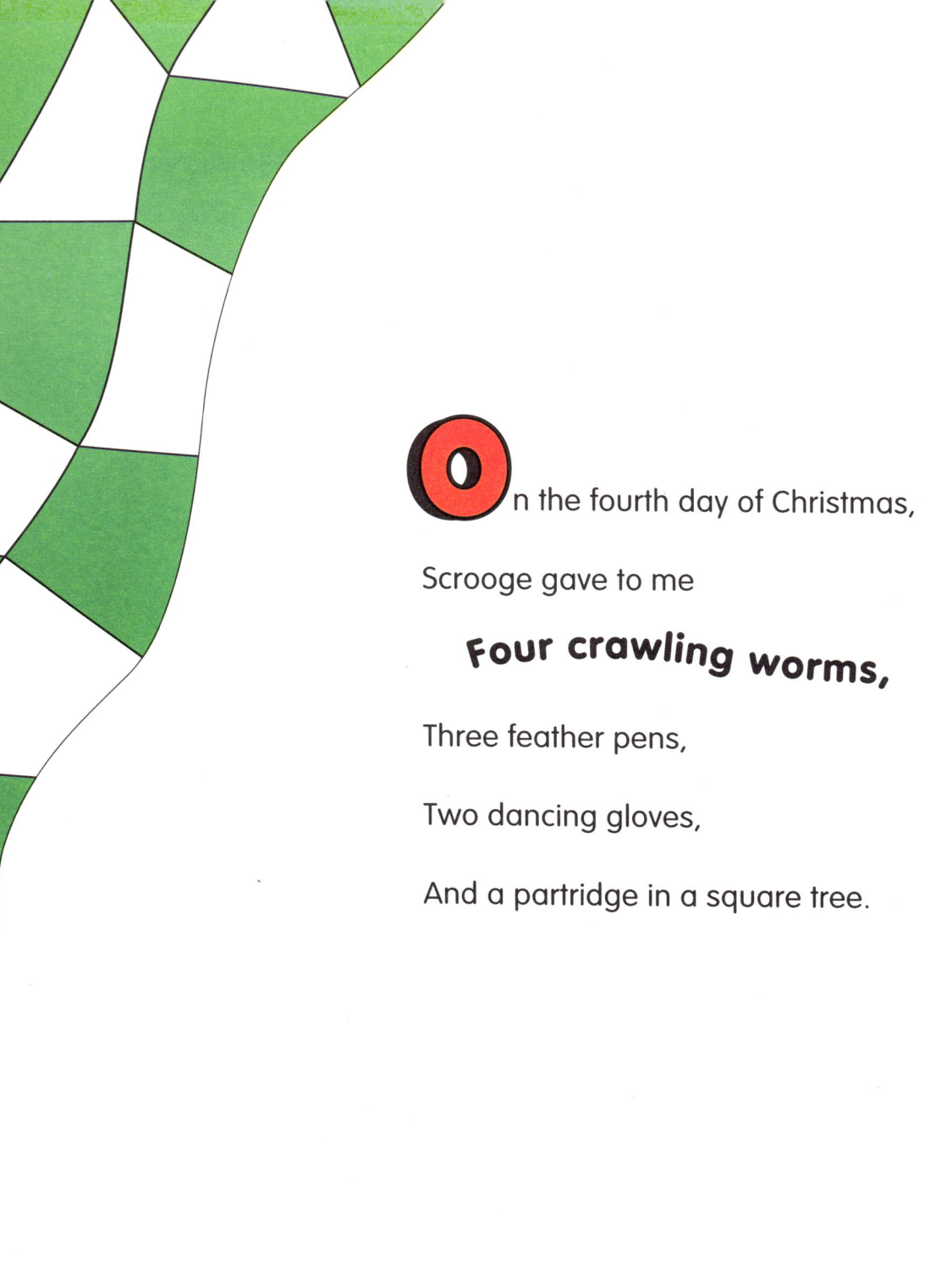

On the fourth day of Christmas,

Scrooge gave to me

Four crawling worms,

Three feather pens,

Two dancing gloves,

And a partridge in a square tree.

On the fifth day of Christmas,

Morty gave to me

Five windup things,

Four crawling worms,

Three feather pens,

Two dancing gloves,

And a partridge in a square tree.

On the sixth day of Christmas,

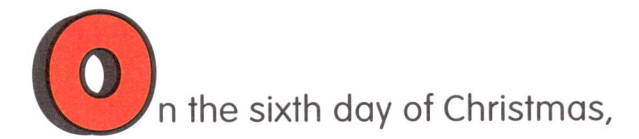

Ferdie gave to me

Six cars a-zooming,

Five windup things,

Four crawling worms,

Three feather pens,

Two dancing gloves,

And a partridge in a square tree.

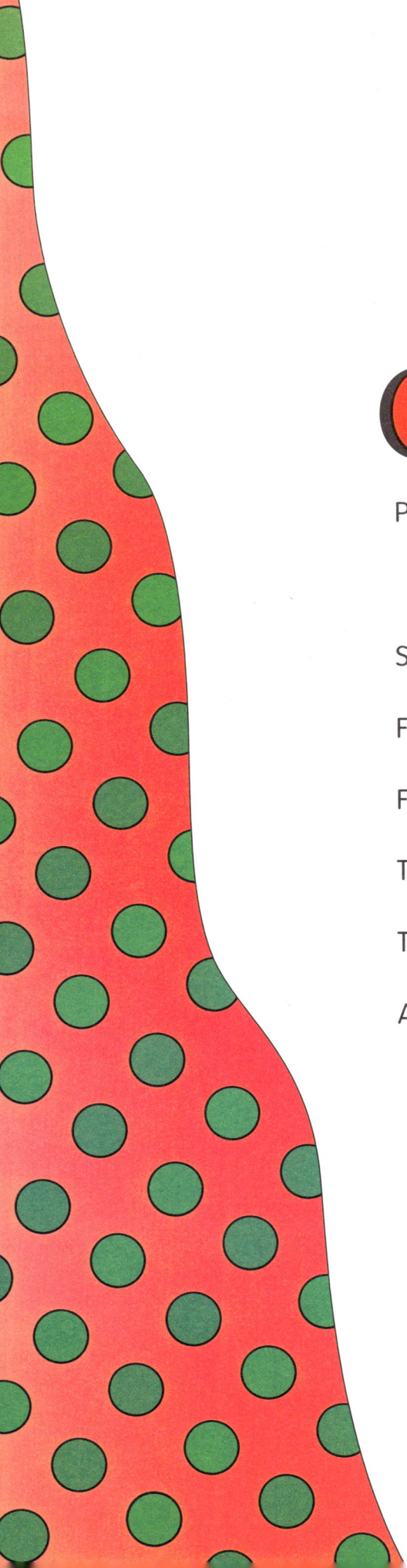

On the seventh day of Christmas,

Pluto gave to me

Seven balls a-bouncing,

Six cars a-zooming,

Five windup things,

Four crawling worms,

Three feather pens,

Two dancing gloves,

And a partridge in a square tree.

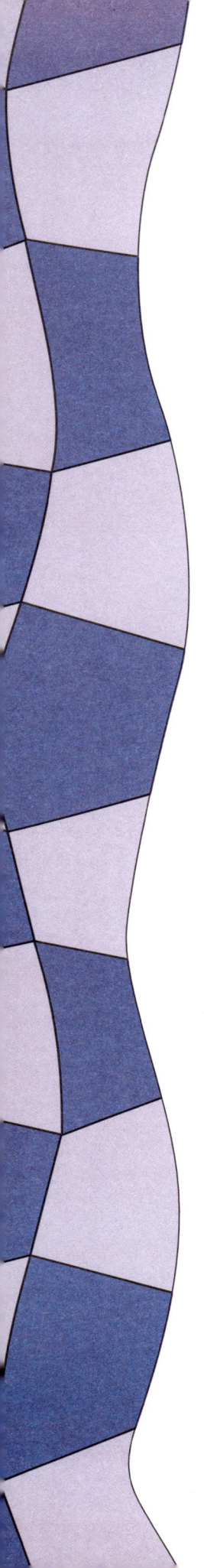

On the eighth day of Christmas,

Daisy gave to me

Eight flowers singing,

Seven balls a-bouncing,

Six cars a-zooming,

Five windup things,

Four crawling worms,

Three feather pens,

Two dancing gloves,

And a partridge in a square tree.

On the ninth day of Christmas,

Huey gave to me

Nine spiders spinning,

Eight flowers singing,

Seven balls a-bouncing,

Six cars a-zooming,

Five windup things,

Four crawling worms,

Three feather pens,

Two dancing gloves,

And a partridge in a square tree.

On the tenth day of Christmas,

Dewey gave to me

Ten brooms a-sweeping,

Nine spiders spinning,

Eight flowers singing,

Seven balls a-bouncing,

Six cars a-zooming,

Five windup things,

Four crawling worms,

Three feather pens,

Two dancing gloves,

And a partridge in a square tree.

On the eleventh day of Christmas,

Louie gave to me

Ten brooms a-sweeping,

Nine spiders spinning,

Eight flowers singing,

Seven balls a-bouncing,

Six cars a-zooming,

Five windup things,

Four crawling worms,

Three feather pens,

Two dancing gloves,

And a partridge in a square tree.

On the twelfth day of Christmas,

friends all gave to me

Twelve drums a-drumming,

Eleven bells a-ringing,

Ten brooms a-sweeping,

Nine spiders spinning,

Eight flowers singing,

Seven balls a-bouncing,

Six cars a-zooming,

Five windup things,

Four crawling worms,

Three feather pens,

Two dancing gloves,

And a partridge in a square tree.

Merry Christmas!